Amazon Prime

Tips and Tricks to Get the Most Out
Of Your Amazon Prime Membership,
How to Join Amazon Prime

MARK HOWARD

Table of Contents

Text Copyright © Mark Howard

Legal & Disclaimer

The content and information contained in this book has been compiled from sources deemed reliable, and it is accurate to the best of the Author's knowledge, information and belief. However, the Author cannot guarantee its accuracy and validity and cannot be held liable for any errors and/or omissions. Further, changes are periodically made to this book as and when needed. Where appropriate and/or necessary, you must consult a professional (including but not limited to your doctor, attorney, financial advisor or such other professional advisor) before using any of the suggested remedies, techniques, or information in this book.

Upon using the contents and information contained in this book, you agree to hold harmless the Author from and against any damages, costs, and expenses, including any legal fees potentially resulting from the application of any of the information provided by this book. This disclaimer applies to any loss, damages or injury caused by the use and application, whether directly or indirectly, of any advice or information presented, whether for breach of contract, tort, negligence, personal injury, criminal intent, or under any other cause of action.

You agree to accept all risks of using the information presented inside this book.

You agree that by continuing to read this book, where appropriate and/or necessary, you shall consult a professional (including but not limited to your doctor, attorney, or financial advisor or such other advisor as needed) before using any of the suggested remedies, techniques, or information in this book.

Introduction

Congratulations on downloading *Amazon Prime: Tips and Tricks to Get the Most Out Of Your Amazon Prime Membership, How to Join Amazon Prime* and thank you for doing so. This is an excellent guide for those who are considering signing up for Amazon Prime as well as for people who would like to learn how to get the most from their current Amazon Prime membership.

The following chapters will discuss what exactly Amazon Prime is and what features are included with your membership. Amazon Video, a feature included with your Prime membership, and how this streaming video service compares with Netflix and Hulu as well as tips and tricks on how to use the service are detailed. How to maximize the use of Amazon Music and how it compares with services such as Spotify and Pandora are also covered.

How and why you should use Amazon's photo storage benefit to store your photos are also discussed along with some other benefits of Amazon Prime that you should know about including Prime Pantry, Prime Wardrobe, Twitch Prime, Prime Outfit Compare and Prime Exclusive Deals.

Tricks and hacks to maximize the amount of money that you save through Amazon Prime and how to make the most out of all your Prime benefits and services are also included.

Additionally, the best (and the cheapest) way for you to sign up for an Amazon Prime Membership and the different types of memberships that are available are outlined.

There are plenty of books on this subject on the market, so thanks again for choosing this one! Every effort was made to ensure it is full of as much useful information as possible. Please enjoy!

Chapter 1: What is Amazon Prime?

Amazon Prime is a paid subscription service that is offered by Amazon.com. Amazon began offering this service in 2005, but since then, it has evolved and expanded into a much more useful International service with over 100 million users.

The cornerstone benefit of Amazon Prime is that registered members receive access to free two-day delivery on Amazon Prime items. The service also has a one-day shipping option and even a same-day option on some items with a minimum purchase amount which is generally $35. The free two-day delivery option, however, does not require a minimum purchase amount, only that the item be an item marked as delivered by Amazon Prime.

Amazon Prime also offers a variety of other Amazon services which, either you do not have access to or are more expensive if you do not have the Prime membership. For example, in addition to the two-day delivery, Amazon Prime offers a video streaming service which rivals well-known video subscription services such as Netflix and Hulu. This streaming video service, although free with a Prime membership, does include in-app purchases which can significantly enhance the user's experience and even allow it to serve as a replacement for cable and other video streaming services.

Amazon Music, a streaming music service provided for free for Prime members, rivals the free versions of Spotify and other popular music streaming services; moreover, if you would like to upgrade to an Amazon music streaming service that rivals the paid versions of services such as Pandora and Tidal, Prime members get a discount on Amazon Music Unlimited.

Amazon Prime also provides its members with Prime Reading, Prime Pantry, Prime Now, Twitch Prime, Amazon Fresh, Prime at Whole Foods Market, access to exclusive brands and deals only for Prime members, Amazon First Reads, and Amazon Rewards. Although you may have to pay an additional fee to access some of these features, they are all offered through Amazon Prime and require an active subscription.

When the optional additional features do have a separate monthly subscription, it is often reduced for Prime members. One example of this is the aforementioned Amazon Music Unlimited. Although Amazon Music Unlimited differs for the free Amazon Prime Music that you receive when you subscribe to Prime in that it is far more extensive, Prime members do receive a discount on this Amazon music service as well as several other services that are offered by or affiliated with Amazon Prime.

For items that have not been released yet, Amazon Prime offers Release Day delivery so that members can get these upcoming items delivered to them on the day that they are released. This allows members to receive exciting new products on the day that they come out without waiting in line at a store or worrying that they will be sold out.

Furthermore, Amazon Prime members are allowed to participate in Prime Day, a day in which items from Amazon Prime are sold at special low prices for additional savings. This is akin to a "Black Friday" for Prime members where they receive deep discounts on items, especially those made by Amazon such as the Echo, Kindle, Fire TV Stick, and more.

Amazon Prime allows members to save money everyday on hot deals by allowing them to get in on the deals 30 minutes before they are open to regular Amazon users. These "Lightening Deals" allow Amazon Prime members to save a significant amount of money, and once they are gone, they are gone. This is just another great way to save money if you know how to maximize your use of your Amazon Prime membership.

Chapter 2: Understanding the Features That Are Included With Your Amazon Prime Membership

All about Amazon Prime Shipping

The primary feature that Amazon Prime offers is fast and free shipping on over 100 million items according to Amazon.

With a paid membership, you enjoy the benefit of having your items shipped to you within two days if they are being shipping by Amazon Prime. Furthermore, whether an item ships through Amazon Prime is clearly denoted with both wording and the prime checkmark symbol so that you do not have to try to figure out which items are shipped by Prime and qualify for the two-day shipping and which items do not. Additionally, although two-day shipping generally means two business days, some items are delivered on Saturday and even Sunday; you can see the exact delivery date on the checkout page.

With Prime, two-day shipping may be fast, but there actually are some quicker options which may even be free. Some items qualify for one-day shipping with a minimum order of $35, and some items can even be shipped and arrive on the same day that they are ordered. For your items to qualify for free one-day shipping, *all* of your items that are used to satisfy the $35 minimum must be eligible for the one-day shipping. This can get a little confusing if you are not familiar with it, and you may be wondering why the one-day shipping option is not available at checkout for an item that stated one-day shipping on its product page. Furthermore, you must place your order before the deadline set for the order to be placed if you want the product delivered the next day. This deadline is shown on both the product page and the checkout page, so you know whether you have placed your order in time or not.

Same-day shipping is also available on some products. You may not be aware that same-day shipping is not the same as Prime Now and may be available on some products even if you don't have Prime Now in your area. Simply look for same day shipping on the products page, reach the minimum amount of $35 of items *all of which qualify for same day shipping*, and order by the deadline which tends to be in the morning.

Prime Now is a faster way of shipping than same-day, and you may be able to receive your items in as little as one to two hours. This service, however, is only available in a few limited zip codes.

Most items that qualify for the free two-day shipping also qualify for *free* return shipping. All you have to do it print out the label and select whether it should be picked up by a carrier or you will drop it off at a locker or the UPS store. You should, of course, check the return policy of the individual item to make sure this is true for your specific item because some items cannot be returned even if they were shipped through Amazon Prime.

No Rush Shipping Option

If you do not need your items which are eligible for prime shipping in a rush, you would be wise to choose the Free No Rush Shipping option. No Rush Shipping allows you to receive your items in six business days instead of two-day shipping. And while you will not get your items in two days as with the traditional Prime delivery option, you will get perks and rewards for waiting on these items.

The rewards you earn from using No Rush Shipping can be applied toward a variety of other things throughout the Amazon site. The rewards can be used towards the purchase of eBooks, Amazon Videos, Prime Pantry essentials, and more. To let you know what you can spend your Amazon rewards bucks on, Amazon sends an email to Prime members detailing their rewards and how they can be redeemed when their No Rush Shipping order ships.

If you are interested in exactly how much your No Rush Shipping benefits are on a particular order, the rewards are listed under that shipping option at checkout. The amount of the reward varies with different orders, so be sure to take a look at exactly what you will receive in return before choosing this option. You may also have the option of choosing to receive a discount at check out; thus, make sure you take the time to look at all of the options for what you may receive if you choose No Rush Shipping because you may be able to choose between a reward and a discount on the same product.

Amazon Prime even keeps track of your No Rush Rewards balance so that you can see how many rewards dollars you have racked up.

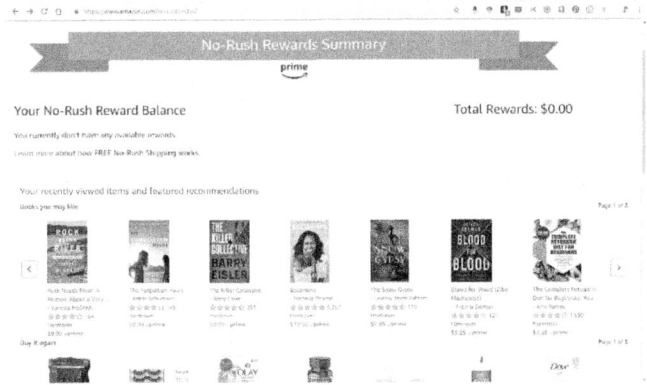

The delivery date for No Rush Shipments is listed, so you do not have to wonder when your items will arrive. Oftentimes, you even receive your items before the delivery date listed. So, if you do not need your items immediately, why no enjoy some of the No Rush Shipping benefits.

Prime Now

Prime Now is a hot feature that Amazon Prime offers from which you can receive items within one to two hours. However, it is only offered in certain areas. This service which is generally only available in major cities such as Atlanta, Austin, Baltimore, Chicago, Dallas, Miami, Nashville, Portland, San Antonio, Seattle, and Tampa along with a few cities outside of the United States. Find out more information about Prime Now here: https://www.amazon.com/primeinsider/tips/prime-now-qa.html?ref=insider_homepage.

Amazon Video, Amazon Music, and Amazon Photo

Amazon Video, Amazon Music, and Amazon Photo are significant features that each deserve their own chapters. However, I will briefly mention them in this chapter. Amazon offers a streaming video service with your Prime membership which is free for you to use, but it does have additional purchases in the app which you may want to consider to fully enjoy your use of the video service and get the most value out of it. Prime also offers a free music service which is a limited version of its Amazon Music Unlimited Service, the paid music streaming service which is offered through Amazon. Prime also offers its members Amazon Photo, a means of storing their photos on the Amazon Photo cloud so that they can free up space on their device while keeping their photos safe and secure.

Exclusive Deals

Amazon Prime often offers its members exclusive deals and perks to help make their membership worth it. Some of the deals that Amazon Prime is offering right now include: Saving Up to 50% on Prime Video, 25% off First Pet Food Purchase, Get a $10 Credit With Select Video Game Pre-orders, Get Three Free Audiobooks When You Sign Up for Audible and Get 20% off Amazon Music.

These exclusive deals are a great way to help you save money and get more out of your Amazon Prime membership, however, if you are like many people who have a Prime membership, you may not have ever checked to see what exclusive deals you have access to. Simply click on the Amazon prime logo at the top left of your screen after you have signed in to your Amazon account. This is where you can find links to many of the goodies that Amazon prime is offering, including "Trending Deals," which have a timer under them to let you know when they expire if you fail to take advantage of them.

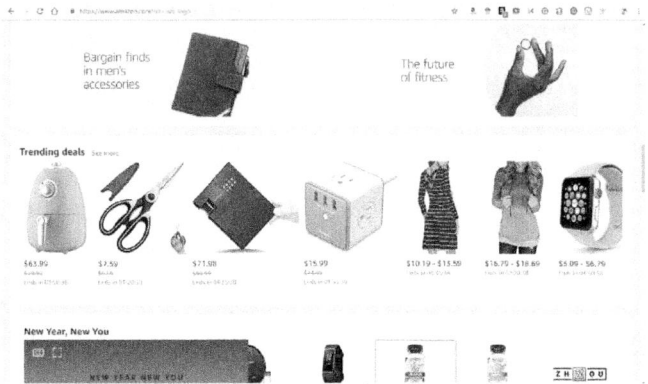

You may want to check out these trending deals once or twice a day on your lunch or coffee break, and you may find some really great deals on some significantly discounted items; remember, though, that these discounts do not last long on most of the deal items.

Other Perks Features and Services

Amazon Prime offers a number of other perks, benefits, and services of which members may want to take advantage, some of which will be covered later in this book. Many of these features are for increased convenience such as Amazon's In-Car delivery, which allows you to have packages delivered to you and place in the trunk of your car or otherwise inside the car. This is a great feature if you do not want your packages left outside.

Amazon Key is also available for Prime members who want to have their packages delivered in the front door of their home. Amazon will install a keyless entry device system that you can monitor through an app on your mobile device; with Amazon Key, you not only get your packages delivered inside your home, but also, you don't have to worry about being locked out. Visit: https://www.amazon.com/b?ie=UTF8&node =17861200011 to find out more about Amazon Key and its In-Home and In-Car delivery.

Amazon also offers a way for you to try clothes and other items in your home for a week before you pay for them through its service called Prime Wardrobe which is covered in a later chapter in this book. You can also receive free fashion advice about what outfit looks best on you with Amazon's new Prime Outfit Compare which also will be cover in great detail as you keep reading.

Chapter 3: Amazon Prime Video

Amazon Prime Video is one of the exciting benefits of Amazon Prime that you are probably already aware exists, however, there is a good chance that you may not be aware of all of the benefits and features that come along with this feature.

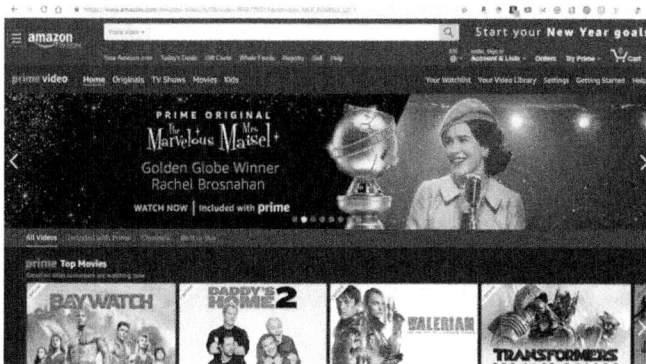

One of the main benefits of Amazon's streaming video service is that it can allow you to save money on your cable bill by providing you with many of the shows that you may find on cable for a much lower price that what you would typically pay for cable service.

What Comes with Prime Video?

Amazon Prime Video offers many of the same things as other video streaming services. The service boasts that it offers thousands of popular television shows and movies for free because they are included in the service. In my estimation it is more like a few hundred television shows and movies that are provided for free with your Amazon Prime subscription, however, it is still a significant number of them. The good news is, however, that the free Prime movies change after a short period of time so if a movie that you want to see is not free on Prime this month, it may be free the next month.

Prime also offers Prime originals, shows that are made exclusively for Amazon Prime and are not available from other services. Some of these shows are very popular so if you want to catch them, you at least need to have an Amazon Prime Video subscription. Some Prime Original shows include: Catastrophe, The Man in the High Castle, Bosch, The Marvelous Mrs. Maisel, All or Nothing, Mozart in the Jungle, Fleabag, Transparent, Sneaky Pete, The Tick, Red Oaks, Hand of God, The Grand Tour, One Mississippi, Eat the World with Emeril Lagasse, Mad Dogs, Doctor Thorne, and Jean-Claude Van Johnson. If you are a fan of any of these shows or the actors in them, you may want to consider getting an Amazon Prime subscription because these shows are free with the basic Prime membership.

In addition to the Amazon Originals which are free with you Amazon Prime subscription and other free shows and movies, Amazon Prime also has a number of television shows that you can purchase individually or the entire season. To be frankly honest, these are the more popular network shows as very few shows that are popular on other networks are actually free on Amazon Video, however, many of the shows that you have to pay for are not available on other streaming services, at least not for free. You will save a little money, however, if you get a season pass to these shows up front instead of paying for the episodes individually. Furthermore, these shows tend to appear approximately the same if you purchase the SD version as they do with HD and the SD episodes are always cheaper if you are interested in saving money.

Amazon Video also lets you rent episodes of some shows for as little as 99 cents per episode. This will save you a little money if you don't feel the need to watch the episode more than once so be sure to check out all available viewing options for the shows you want to watch.

Add-On Channels

Amazon Prime Video also allows you to select some add-on channels such as Starz, Showtime, Cinemax, Lifetime Movie Channel, HBO and more for an additional monthly fee which is determined by which individual add-on channels you choose. This is a huge perk for people who have had the experience of choosing a cable bundle that does not have the channels that you want or paying too much for a cable bundle with extra channels that you never watch. There are over 100 premium channels to choose from and with Prime Video, you choose just the add-on channels that you want and some of these channels are as low as $3.99 a month. Furthermore, you can cancel one or more of these channels at any time without having to change or lose your service. Thus, if you do not have a lot of time to spend watching television and you are seeking to save money on your cable bill, Amazon Prime Video is a great option.

Movies that Prime does not offer for free can often either be rented and the rental price is much cheaper than buying the movie. Moreover, there is often a choice of additional ways to purchase. Sometimes the movie is offered though add-on channels which have a free trial, is a low-cost channel, or may be a free channel which you may want to subscribe to. Therefore, it is always wise to check out the additional ways to purchase before deciding to buy or rent a film.

Watch Prime Anywhere

Amazon Prime is compatible with a large number of devices. You can watch you Prime Videos on compatible Smart Televisions, with Fire TV, on gaming consoles, tablets, and phones through the Amazon Prime Video app. On many of your devices, you can download the videos that you have purchased so that you can watch them offline.

Quality

Prime Video offers great resolution for its videos. You can use 4K Ultra HD with Prime to experience spectacular color and contrast along with very crisp pictures. Moreover, some movies and shows offer X-ray access which takes you behind the scenes of the shows and gives you additional information about the filming and its characters which gives you a more 'insider' viewing experience.

How Does Amazon Prime Video Compare with Hulu and Netflix?

There is no disputing the fact that Hulu and Netflix are considered to be two of the top video streaming giants, but Amazon Prime Video holds up pretty well when it is compared to these two services and has quickly become one of the top video streaming giants in own right. All three of these streaming services, Netflix, Hulu, and Amazon Prime Video, provide consumers with on demand videos and content are a very reasonable price, however, there are some ways that Prime Video differs from these services.

Amazon Prime Video is included with a Prime subscription membership which offers free two-day shipping and other benefits whereas both Hulu and Netflix are stand alone video streaming services which do not offer other features besides live television, DVR, and on demand videos. Amazon Prime Video, However, can be purchased as a stand-alone video streaming service as well for $8.99 a month. This is only one dollar more than Hulu's most basic plan in which its on demand videos come with commercials. Amazon, on the other hand, does not have commercials in its shows, however, many of these shows have to be purchased for an additional fee whereas Hulu offers all of its shows for free with a paid subscription. But due to the extra fee that Amazon charges for these shows, many of the shows on Amazon are from more recent seasons than the shows on Hulu and Netflix as well. In fact, some of the shows you can watch on Amazon Video, you can't even find on Netflix and Hulu.

It is important to note, however, that Amazon Video is available on fewer streaming devices that Netflix and Hulu. While you can get both Netflix and Hulu on Chromecast and Chromecast Ultra, Amazon Video is currently unavailable from these devices. Thus, it is important to check to see if your device is compatible with Amazon Video.

It is also important to note that if you ever choose to cancel your Prime membership you *still* have access to all of the content that you purchased from Amazon Prime Video through the Prime Video app. This mean that you do not lose this content simply because you cancelled your membership.

Chapter 4: Amazon Prime Music

Amazon Prime Music is included with the Amazon Prime subscription and boasts that it includes over 2 million hand curated songs which you can stream. In addition, the service offers playlists that are tailored directly to you and personalized stations which you can listen to, so you do not ever have to search too hard to find the music that you love.

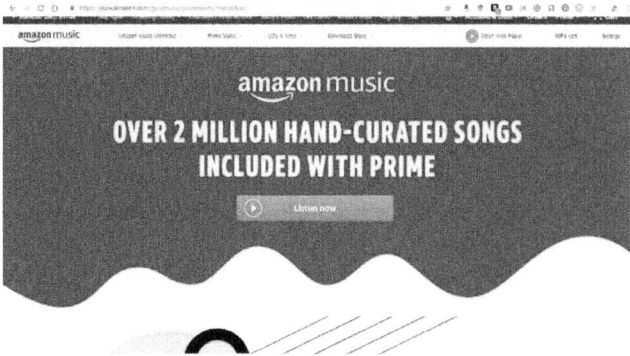

A great thing about Amazon Prime Music is that it is compatible with a number of different devices. Some of the devices with which you can use Amazon Prime Music are Echo devices, Sonos devices, Fire TV devices, iOS devices, Roku devices, Xbox One, Play-Fi devices, Android TV, and more.

Another great thing about Amazon Prime music, one that distinguishes it from services such as Spotify, is that you can download more than one million songs for free from Amazon Prime Music. Most other services either let you download the songs that you pay for individually or you have to pay for a subscription to that particular service to be able to download songs. Thus, if you would like to download some songs and take them on the go with you, this is a great service for you to utilize. And many people may be unaware of this feature or are currently not using it. Amazon Prime Music also beats Spotify's free music offering due to the fact that you can select the specific songs that you want to listen to instead of listening to a shuffle that is selected by the service after you select the first song.

In order to download songs, all you need to do is download the free Amazon Music App. This app only works with mobile devices and is not available for desktops and laptops. But, the mobile devices are great for playing songs on the go. It is important to note that you cannot export the song which you download into the app and you must play them through the app, so as long as you have the mobile device and the app running, you can listen to your downloaded songs on the go without utilizing any of your data.

If you want to play songs on a laptop or desktop, you just stream them from the streaming service. Unfortunately, these songs cannot be played on a desktop or laptop that is offline unless you purchase the songs and download them to these devices so that you can play them when you are not connected to the internet.

Even though you cannot download songs to your computer or laptop, you can import songs to Amazon Prime Music from your computer or laptop. However, the service only allows you to hold 250 songs without having to pay extra.

If you have an Amazon account and an Amazon Prime membership, and you are having trouble being able to use Amazon Prime Music, it is important to make sure that you have a billing address and a 1-Click method of payment entered into your account. This is true even though it is a service that is free with your Amazon Prime subscription.

Amazon Prime Music Differs from Amazon Music Unlimited

It is very important to note that Amazon Prime Music is not actually the same as Amazon Music Unlimited. Amazon Music Unlimited is a music streaming service by Amazon which was designed to compete with the likes of Pandora, Tidal, and several other major music apps that offer paid subscriptions. Likewise, Unlimited is a paid subscription service provided for the price of $7.99 a month with a Prime membership and which offers users access to 50 million songs on demand and always free of any ads. The service also allows users to listen offline with unlimited skips. Furthermore, Unlimited has new music and newly released albums; new music is often hard to find with the free Prime Music service. The cost of Amazon Music Unlimited is only slightly more if you do not have a Prime membership; it is $9.99 for all users who are not members of Amazon Prime. However, for those of you who really like music, it is good to know that you get a discount with your Prime membership and the free version, Amazon Prime Music, allows you to try it out and get a feel for it before deciding whether or not to upgrade to Unlimited.

If you have both a Prime membership and an Amazon Echo, you can get Amazon Music Unlimited for only $3.99 a month. This is probably the best value when you consider the fact that the Amazon Echo is currently selling on the site for $29.99 and it can be used for other things, not simply for playing music. There is also a $4.99 Student Plan and a Family Plan if you would like to consider these options.

The size of Amazon Music Unlimited is as such that it is a much better version of Prime Music, one where you can find all of the songs that you want, and you do not have to worry about ads. It also offers a 90-day free trial before you start getting charged for the service. Thus, this service is still useful to Amazon Prime members who have access to free Amazon Prime Music.

And if you just want to stream a little bit of music, Amazon Prime Music is still the way to go. The best thing about this music streaming service is that it is free with your paid subscription to Amazon Prime. So, if you do not need to have access to a lot of music, then this is definitely your cheapest option for a quality music streaming service.

Chapter 5: Amazon Prime Photo

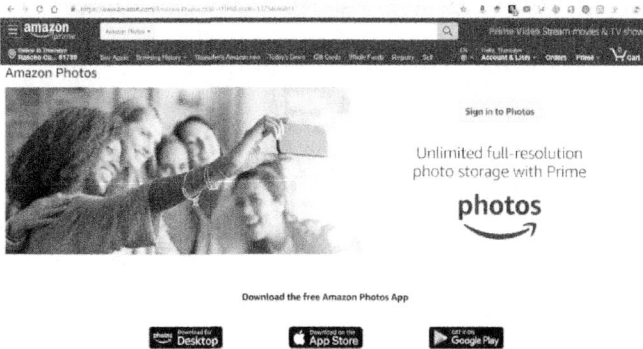

Another great feature that Amazon Prime offers its members is unlimited photo storage. This is a very important feature for people who have lots of photos but do not want to use up all of the storage space of their digital devices to store the photos. And best of all, these photos can be stored at full resolution at their original quality so that you do not have to sacrifice any of the quality to store lots of photos with Amazon; this is an important feature due to the fact that many similar photo storage options compress the photos, resulting in lower quality photos than the original version.

To store photos with Amazon Photo Storage, simply download the Amazon Photos app (which can be found at https://www.amazon.com/Amazon-Photos/b?ie=UTF8&node=13234696011).

Amazon Photos is easy to use, and it backs up all of your photos. All you have to do is download the app, open it, and turn on the auto-save feature, and the app will back up all of your photos. After all of your photos have been saved in the Amazon Photos cloud, there is no longer a need to store them on your phone. You can free up some of your device's storage space by deleting the photos that are saved to the device, and you will still have all of your photo safely saved to the Amazon Photo cloud.

One great feature about Amazon Photos is its search feature. Instead of being forced to scroll through unlimited numbers of photos, you can simply use the search function to do a more targeted search so that you can pull up exactly the photo that you are looking for.

In addition, Amazon Photos allows you to share photos with friends and family easily. You can even pool your photos with family and friends so that all of your loved ones can keep your photos together in a group. One feature, the Family Vault, allows you to invite family members to share photos with you in the Family Vault and as an additional benefit, each member of your Family Vault receives their own Amazon Photos account with up to 5 GB of storage space for photos and videos.

Furthermore, you can display your photos on your Fire Tv and a number of other compatible devices so that you can look at all of your photos on the big screen. You can even enjoy slideshows of your photos.

Moreover, Amazon Prime Photos allows you to easily order prints with just a few clicks in the app. This means that if you decide that you would like a physical copy of one of your photos at any time, all you have to do is click on the photo and order as many prints as you need, and they will be sent to you. You do, of course, have to pay for the prints, but prints could not be easier or more convenient to order than they are with the Prime Photos app. And if you have a photo printer, you can actually print your photos out directly from your computer without having to pay for any prints. That's great for people who have a lot of photos.

Chapter 6: More Benefits of Amazon Prime That You Should Know

Amazon Family

Almost everyone that knows anything about Amazon Prime knows about Amazon Video and Amazon Music, but you may still not be aware of a benefit of Prime known as Prime Family. This does not mean that this is not a very valuable benefit.

Tell us about your little one to start receiving exclusive discounts, parenting tips via email newsletter, and more

family

Whether you're expecting, raising a toddler, or navigating the tween years, tell us about your kids to receive exclusive discounts, parenting tips, and much more - just for your family

• Email newsletter with parenting tips, product recommendations, and exclusive deals
• Up to 20% off diapers, baby food, & more
• 15% Baby Registry completion discount

Amazon Family gives you a lot of great deals and benefits on items for the household. Furthermore, you can get some great discounts on certain items that Amazon deems to be for the family. (You can find more information on Amazon Family here: https://www.amazon.com/gp/help/custome r/display.html?nodeId=201895020)

Amazon Dash

Amazon offers convenient Amazon Dash buttons that can be used to order common household goods that you need to restock quickly. You can actually order goods at the push of a button using these little things that you can stick where you need them. For instance, you can place a Gain Laundry Detergent button in the laundry room so that you can conveniently order more laundry detergent when you need it without having to log in to your Amazon account or even leave the laundry room.

Early Access to Deals

One great thing about Amazon Prime is that it offers you early access to some great deals simply for being a member. Thus, you get to order sale items before the rest of Amazon's users which helps to ensure that these items will be in stock for you and you'll get yours even if they do not get theirs.

Prime Pantry

Amazon Prime members also have access to Prime Pantry, which is an Amazon service that allows you to order packaged food and household essentials without having to purchase them in bulk. You simply have to fill up a box with a set number of items before the Prime Pantry box qualifies for shipment. There is an additional fee involved as this feature is no completely complementary with Amazon Prime. However, the additional fee is minimal. If you plan to use Prime Pantry, you may want to pay the additional fee of $4.99 which allow you to have all Prime Pantry orders over $40 shipped to your door for free. If you do not plan to use Prime Pantry regularly, you can simply play a flat fee of $7.99 for each order and forgo the monthly subscription to Prime Pantry. Either way, you have to have a subscription to

Amazon Prime to use the Prime Pantry service at all.

Prime Reading

Prime Reading allows Prime members to borrow up to ten books at a time and read them either on a Kindle device or in the Kindle app. Magazines are also available and can be borrowed for free. You can never have more than 10 books out at a time, and you don't get to keep the books and magazines, but it is great to get a chance to read through them for free. The selection of books that are available is a little smaller than the selection that you will find in the Kindle Lending Library. However, it is still a great selection where you have tons to choose from.

Amazon Restaurants

Amazon Restaurants is only available in certain areas, however, in the areas in which it is available, it is a great service for people who would like restaurant meals delivered to their home instead of fast food and pizza. If you live in approximately 17 major cities across the United States such as New York City, Los Angeles, or Orlando, you can get food delivered for a number of your local restaurants through your Amazon Prime membership if you place a minimum order of $20. To see if you can take advantage of this service in your area, simply log in to your account and scroll down to the very bottom of the screen and right above the "Conditions of Use" link, you will see Amazon Restaurants in the last column.

Amazon Elements

Did you know that Amazon recently came out with its own brand of products? This brand is known as Amazon Elements, and it is available exclusively to Amazon Prime members. The line boasts that it offers premium products of transparent origins. Some of the products that are offered include vitamins and baby wipes. Make sure you clip the coupons on the Amazon Elements page and use Subscribe and Save for any items that you regularly need to gain additional savings. These are great deals even if the selection of products is limited!!!

Amazon Prime Wardrobe

Amazon Prime recently added a new Prime feature which should be exciting to all of those who like to shop for clothes online.

Prime Wardrobe allows Amazon Prime members to select certain clothing and accessory items, have them shipped to your home and try them out for a week without paying anything. If you like the items and decide to keep them, you do have to pay for them; however, if you decide that the items you have selected are not for you, they come in a resealable box with a pre-printed return label so that you can conveniently return them.

Amazon Prime and Whole Foods

Amazon Prime offers its members discounts at Whole Foods Markets. Prime members get an Additional 10% off of items that are on sale in this store. The store's customers who are members of Amazon Prime also get discounts on weekly sale items.

Amazon Prime Outfit Compare

Recently Amazon Prime launched a new free service for its Prime members call Prime Outfit Compare which allows Prime members to upload photos of yourself wearing two different outfits to get advice on the best outfit for them.

You must upload the photos through the app, and an Amazon fashion specialist will give you advice on which outfit is the best one for you. It only takes a minute or two to receive a response, and the response takes into account such things such as the latest trends, how the outfit fits you and the best colors for you. This is a great feature that you may want to try on date night or if you have a job interview, especially since it is free, and it only takes a few minutes. It's like receiving a knowledgeable friend's free advice right on what to wear, right in the comfort of your home.

Amazon Warehouse Deals

Even though Amazon has some pretty good prices already, you can find some great deals in its Outlet Store section as well as in its Warehouse Section. Items sold from Amazon's Warehouse are an open box which often allows the purchaser to receive a significant discount over the "new" new items listed on Amazon. You may not want to order an item that you want to arrive in its perfect new condition due to this feature, but if you can stand a few nicks and scratches, taking advantage of Warehouse deals can help you save money, and you may be able to get the item through your Prime membership. It states under many of the items in the Warehouse that some options are Prime eligible.

Twitch Prime

Gamers should be excited to know that Prime has something for them too. If you are a paying member of Amazon Prime, you receive a free subscription to Twitch Prime. Twitch Prime subscriptions normally cost $4.99 a month or more depending on what plan you get, but with Prime, you can forgo the additional monthly fee and enjoy a gaming channel for free.

Twitch is a gamers streaming service. With a Twitch subscription, you send a recurring payment to one of the channels on that service to support the gamer on that service for continued streaming of that particular channel. When you subscribe, you receive a status boost in the gamer's chat room which provides you with new emotes as well as other digital goodies that gamers enjoy. You are also able to view your Twitch channel without the ads that are traditionally present for those who do not have a subscription.

If you already have a membership to Twitch but not Amazon Prime, you can sign up for Prime from the Twitch website by clicking on the words "Twitch Prime" near the top left of the screen on the twitch home page. This will help to ensure that your Twitch account and your Amazon Prime account are linked up so that you can enjoy the benefits of a free Twitch channels subscription with your prime membership.

If you signed up for Amazon first, from your Amazon Prime account, you need to unlock twitch prime in order to link the two accounts and enjoy the benefits you are entitled to on Twitch for being a Prime member. To do this, you need to make sure that you are logged into both your Amazon prime account and your Twitch account at the same time in the same browser. From your Amazon account, use the drop-down search bar and scroll all the way to video games which is at the very bottom and insert Twitch Prime in the search bar. Next, click on

Twitch Prime which appears near the top of the screen in purple. This will take you to a screen that gives you the option to connect your Twitch account.

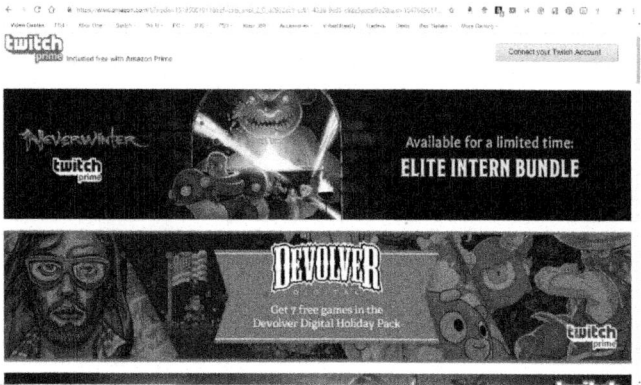

Click on this bar to link the two accounts. Follow the instruction and click "Confirm" to link the account; now, your Amazon Prime and Twitch accounts are linked on all of your devices on which you use either of these accounts. This makes it easy for you to enjoy all of the benefits and rewards that you are due on Twitch for being an Amazon prime member.

It is important to note that you cannot enjoy the benefit of subscribing to a Twitch channel for free during your Amazon Prime free trial period. You must, in fact, be a paying member of Amazon Prime which occurs after your free trial period ends. So, wait until you Amazon free trial has ended to go to the Twitch channel you wish to subscribe to and click the "Subscribe" button that appears on the page. You will see a variety of subscription options including "Free Channel Sub With Twitch Prime." Choose this option. One other thing to note, you must redo this step once a month for the duration of your Amazon Prime subscription because, although you are offered the Free Twitch Prime subscription every month, it does not automatically renew, and you must re-click the "Subscribe Free" button every month. You don't need to be concerned about losing your subscription or information so long as you take this step to renew your subscription within 30-days of your lack free subscription expiring.

Additionally, since your free Twitch subscription on that channel must be renewed every month, at the end of a month, you can actually choose to renew your subscription on another channel. Thus, if you have gotten your fill of one channel and want to try another one, you are free to do so every 30 days.

For those who already have a paid subscription to a Twitch channel and would like to switch using Amazon Prime's free

Twitch subscription benefit, all you have to do is go to your account and select "Don't renew." You will still have the paid subscription until the end of that allotted month. After this paid subscription runs out, make sure that your Amazon account and your Twitch account are connected and select the free Prime subscription option on the same channel.

There are a few other benefits that you get when you link your Prime and Twitch accounts that you may want to be aware of some that you do not miss out on these gamer goodies. As a Prime member, you get free Twitch games every month, which you should be sure to claim. In addition, you have access to some free in-game extras, emoticons, a Prime chat badge, and more.

You can find out about these prime extras and more by visiting twitch.tv./prime.

Chapter 7: Tricks and Hacks to Maximize Your Savings with Amazon Prime

The Extended Free Trial

Many people are not aware that they can actually be offered the opportunity to extend the free trial. There is no guarantee that Amazon with offer you an extension but it happens from time to time. One way that you may be offered an extension on your free trial is to check out all of the benefits of prime but cancel the membership before the end of the free trial. When you look through the Prime benefits again, you may be offered a pop-up window which asks you if you want to extend your free trial for another month.

That means that you get two free months before you start paying for the service.

There is no guaranteed time in which Amazon Prime offers this option that I am aware of or any minimum amount of purchases that must have been made. Furthermore, this option may not be offered before your free trial expires and you are unable to use your benefits. (Oftentimes, it may be offered to get you to come back to Prime after your trial period and benefits have ended.) Thus, if your primary concern is not saving money and you would like to keep your Prime benefits going continuously, this may not be the best option for you. However, it is always good to look out for it. You never know when Amazon Prime may offer you another free month.

Sharing Your Amazon Account

Of course, you can probably already figure out how to share your Prime membership with other members of your household, at least the free and expedited shipping benefits; however, sharing prime deserves to be mentioned because Amazon makes it very easy to do while still allowing every member of the household to keep their own account. You can do this through Amazon Households. Amazon Households allows you to link two adults, up to four teens, and up to four children on one account by going to https://www.amazon.com/myh/households and inputting the information for the other members of the household to link them to the Prime member's account. This means that you do not need to have two or three Prime memberships per household and each member of the household gets to keep his or her account exactly how he or she likes it. This is important so that your kids and teens can keep their tailored recommendations for Amazon based on their search history and purchases and you can keep yours.

Your Free Trial of the Washington Post

Yes, your Prime membership does come with a six-month free trial of the Washington Post, one of this country's most respected newspapers. This is a great perk, but you must remember to sign up for it. You may also want to place a note on your calendar to remind you of when your free trial ends so that you will not be surprised to see a charge on your credit card for it if you go past the free trial period.

Make Sure to Use Your Audible Channels for Prime

Yes, Amazon Prime does have a deal with Audible in which members receive a free trial which comes with two free audiobooks, but did you know that some features of Audible are still free to Amazon Prime users even if they do not sign up for the free Audible subscription. That is because there is Audible Channels for Prime which allows Amazon Prime members to listen to a variety of audiobooks, podcasts, and more, all without having to pay anything extra. In fact, there are about 50 different books in these free Audible Channels, and they change regularly. To take advantage of the benefit, you need to download the Audible app to your device and sign in to your Amazon account.

Get a Free Book Every Month

One perk that many people are not aware of that is offered by Amazon Prime is Kindle First. Even many Prime members are not aware of what Kindle First is. In short, it is a way for you to get to download a free book every month from a list of six books that the editors have decided to make available that month. Even if this does not sound like a large selection, the editors try to choose six diverse and interesting titles that readers may be interested in the read. And since it's free, you might as well check out the list and download one book a month that you may want to read later at least.

Kindle Owner's Lending Library

Kindle's Owner's Lending Library is great too for those who want to borrow a few books to check out or read and then return. But, there is one small catch that many people may not be aware of which may cause them to get this feature confused with the Kindle Unlimited paid service. Yes, the Kindle Owner's Lending Library is free to *Kindle Owners*. This means that you must own one of the Kindle devices to take advantage of this benefit. If you do own a Kindle, however, you can select from over 800,000 books. These books are free for you to borrow and you can return them at any time. This means that you do not have to return them within a few days or at the end of the month or you will be charged. And there are a lot of very good book to choose from to borrow for free including past and present best sellers. Thus, if you are an avid reader and you own a Kindle device, this is one benefit that you should be taking advantage of. Simply go to the "Kindle Owner's Lending Library" on your device and located in either the Kindle Store or the Fire Bookstore and choose the "Borrow for Free" option. It's that simple, and it's free!

If You Buy CD's Check to See If you Qualify for A Free One!

If you are a Prime Member and you purchase a CD with your Amazon Prime account, you may qualify to receive the MP3 version of the album that you purchased for free. This free MP3 copy of the album must be played through your Prime Music App; however, it does not make sense not to make sure you get your digital copy. Therefore, you should always be sure to log in to your Prime account when shopping on Amazon if you have one.

Express Shipping???

There is a way to potentially get express shipping on a number of items while only pay for one express shipping, however, this trick is not guaranteed to work all of the time. If you order several different items from Amazon at approximately the same time but in different transactions, and you choose expedited shipping for one, they may ship the other items in the same box with the expedited item, at least if you order these items with the Prime two-day shipping. Now, this is not guaranteed, so don't be disappointed if the expedited item and the other items arrive separately.

A Free Month of Prime for a Late Delivery

This is another perk that is not guaranteed to work. However, it is worth a try. If your

Prime delivery does not arrive on time according to the date that you were given at check out, you may be able to get a free month of Amazon Prime by contacting customer service and voicing a complaint about the late delivery. You may need to ask for a free month extension on your Prime membership. It is best to do this through Amazon customer service's very convenient chat function which has an agent with you in the chat. Although there is no guarantee that you will receive your free month of Prime service, the customer service agents at Amazon are generally good at ensuring customer satisfaction so if you package was late, it's worth a try.

Did You Fail to Cancel an Add-On Channel or Other Addition to Your Prime Membership Before Being Billed for It?

Sometimes, you may want to try one of the add-on channels that you can access through your free Amazon Video membership as many of them offer free trials. If you forget to cancel before the end of the free trial and get billed for it, you can contact Amazon's customer service for a refund of this amount; so long as you have used the channel much since the end of the billing date, Amazon typically will refund you the fee and end the service immediately.

This probably works for several other features that Amazon offers that have monthly subscriptions. It is important to note that for you to receive a refund, Amazon will cancel that service as of that date instead of at the end of the month but if you didn't want or no longer need that particular service or channel, you might as well get your money back. As stated, it is easiest to get a refund through the chat function although phone and email may work as well.

Chapter 8: Signing Up for Amazon Prime

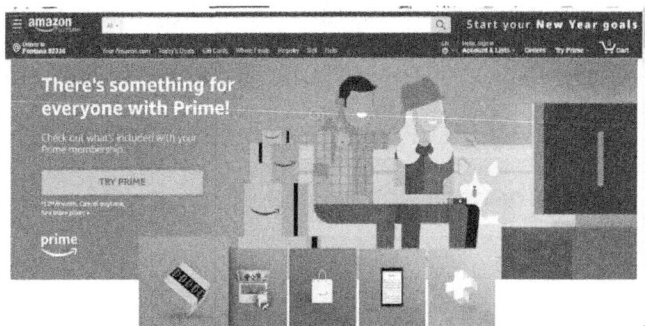

Signing up for Amazon prime is easy to do. Simply click "Try Prime," which is located beside the shopping cart on the top right portion of the screen for those who have an Amazon account and are not Prime members. Upon clicking on "Try Prime," you will be taken to a screen which contains several membership options.

If you do not already have an Amazon account or you are not signed in to your account, you will see three prominent options displayed. The three most prominent options for Prime membership that are offered are a Prime Video membership for $8.99 a month, a Prime Monthly membership for $12.99 a month, and an Annual Prime membership for $119 a year.

Since you have probably never been an Amazon Prime member if you do not have an Amazon account, you do not want to click on any of these three options. Instead, click on the Try Prime bar under the third option. You will then be directed to either sign in to your Amazon account or sign up for an Amazon account.

After either signing in or signing up, you most likely want to select the Start Your 30-Day Free Trial button to avoid paying for your first month of membership. This is the same page that should appear directly from clicking on "Try Prime" if you are already signed in to the account. This is true even if you want to select the Annual Membership option because you can change to an annual membership before the end of your 30-day free trial if you would like to continue with Amazon Prime with an Annual membership.

After clicking "Start Your 30-Day Free Trial," you will be directed to enter a credit card or debit card so that you can be charged at the end of the free trial. You may wish to write down the date the free trial ends on your calendar so that you will not be surprised by a charge on your card. You can also opt to have a reminder sent to your email address three days before the end of the trial.

Different Types of Memberships

In a smaller letter under "Start Your 30-Day Free Trial," is a clickable "more membership options." If you click on this, you will find that the annual membership and the monthly membership are listed. The annual membership works out to $9.92 a month which is several dollars cheaper than the monthly membership for those who have the $119 available at the end of the free trial period and would like to keep their Amazon Prime subscription.

If you are a student or you have a valid EBT/Medicaid card, you will want to select one of these options listed under the Start Your 30-Day Free Trial button.

Student Membership

Unlike with the traditional Amazon prime membership where you get a one-month free trial, if you select an Amazon Student membership, you get a six-month free trial which, of course, you should take advantage of. And even after your free trial ends, you still save money over the traditional Amazon Prime free trial. The monthly membership for the Amazon Student is only $6.49 a month for the monthly subscription and $59 a year which works out to $4.92 a month for the annual subscription. In addition, this membership comes with exclusive college deals and promotions.

To qualify for an Amazon student

membership, you need to have a valid .edu email address. If you are a student registered in at least one course at a college or university in the United States, and you do not have a valid .edu email address, you can provide proof of enrollment to Amazon by providing a scan of photo of either your student ID, your transcript, your tuition bill, or an official acceptance letter. To provide proof of enrollment, please send an e-mail t from the e-mail address associated with your Amazon.com account.

One great way to save money on Amazon Prime for parents and family members of a college student is to share an account with a student with a valid .edu email!

EBT and Medicaid

If you have an EBT or Medicaid card, you can

sign up for an Amazon Prime membership for $5.99 a month after your free trial month. This means that if you are on a tight budget and you have the valid documentation to prove it, you still get to enjoy the benefits of Amazon Prime. Even if you don't order a lot of packages, this deal may be great to take advantage of due to the free video streaming service from Amazon Prime Video which will allow you to save money over Netflix, Hulu, and the like which are paid subscription services.

Give the Gift of Prime

There is also a give the gift of Prime sign up option if you want to give someone Amazon Prime as a gift. If you know someone who is constantly ordering things online and you don't know exactly what to get them, a subscription to Amazon Prime delivered to the person's email inbox is a great gift.

You can even you this option to send yourself the gift of prime to the email address with which you signed up for Amazon. There is a three-month option for $39 if you or someone you know only needs to have Prime for a short period of time but would like to have it for more than a month. Furthermore, you can ask someone to give you the gift of Amazon prime instead of buying you a gift to ensure that you can order the items you want.

Putting Your Membership on Hold and Ending Your Membership

One good thing about Amazon is that it lets you cancel your membership without a hassle. In fact, if you have a monthly membership, you can suspend or cancel your Amazon Prime membership through your account without ever needing to talk to customer service. After you have signed up for Amazon Prime, if you would ever like to cancel your membership or place it on hold for a month or two because your finances are low, simply go to "Your Prime Membership" in the drop-down menu under Accounts & Lists. Once you are there, you will see an option that says, "End Your Prime Membership." Click on this option to end your Prime membership and keep from being charged for the next period. This means that, unlike with many other services which have a contract and a minimum period of membership, if you decide at the end of a month that you no longer want Amazon Prime, you can simply cancel, and you will not be charged further.

Another good thing about Amazon is that after you have canceled your account if you ever want to come back to Amazon Prime, all your information is not lost and is still present in your account.

Conclusion

Thank you for taking the time to read *Amazon Prime: Tips and Tricks to Get the Most Out Of Your Amazon Prime Membership, How to Join Amazon Prime.* I hope that you found the information provided to you in this book to be informative and useful as I have tried to provide you with all the knowledge that you need to make the most of your Amazon Prime membership.

The next step is to go to Amazon.com and sign up for Amazon Prime so that you can start enjoying the benefits of your membership and saving money along the way. Remember that it is always best to start with the free trial membership even if you plan to get a student membership (*especially with that six-month free trial!!!*) or a yearly membership.

Finally, if you found this book useful in any way, a review on Amazon is always appreciated!

Mark Howard

Check Out Other Books

Go here to check out other related books that might interest you:

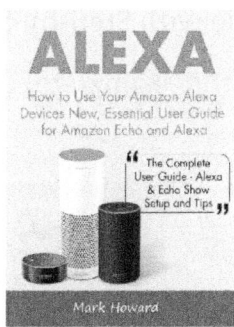

Alexa: How to Use Your Amazon Alexa Devices New, Essential User Guide for Amazon Echo and Alexa (The Complete User Guide-Alexa & Echo Show Setup and Tips)

https://amzn.to/2NuBeFe

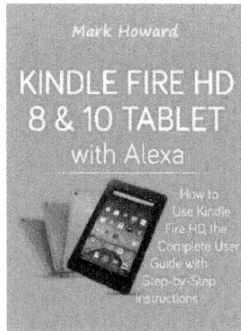

Kindle Fire HD 8 & 10 Tablet with Alexa: How to Use Kindle Fire HD, the Complete User Guide with Step-by-Step Instructions

https://amzn.to/2NMvarM

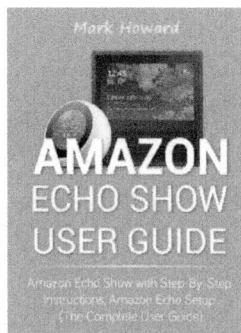

Amazon Echo Show User Guide: Amazon Echo Show with Step-by-Step Instructions, Amazon Echo Setup (The Complete User Guide)

https://amzn.to/2NOSdm7

Fire Stick: Essential User Guide for Amazon
Fire Stick, How to Unlock Your Fire Stick Like
a Pro (Amazon Fire TV, Amazon Fire TV
Stick, Amazon Fire TV Cube)

https://amzn.to/2Mypamo

Amazon Echo Dot - 2nd Generation Amazon Echo Dot with Alexa: How to Unlock the True Potential of Your Echo Dot, Learn to Use Your Echo Dot Like a Pro

https://amzn.to/2KZ6VVL

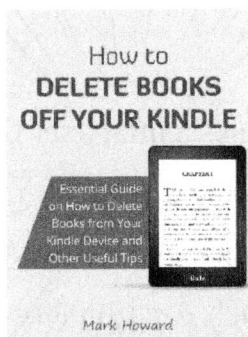

How to Delete Books off Your Kindle: Essential Guide on How to Delete Books from Your Kindle Device and Other Useful Tips

https://amzn.to/2MJl27s

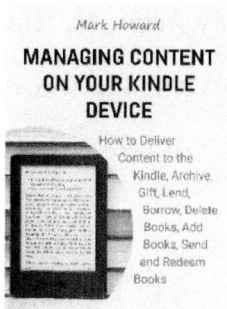

Managing Content on Your Kindle Device:

How to Deliver Content to the Kindle,

Archive, Gift, Lend, Borrow, Delete Books,

Add Books, Send and Redeem Books

https://amzn.to/2RqAgft

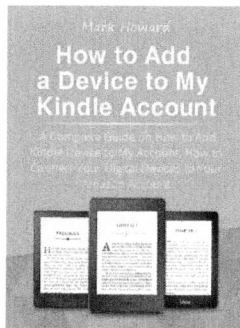

How to Add a Device to My Kindle Account: A

Complete Guide on How to Add Kindle

Device to My Account, How to Connect Your
Digital Devices to Your Amazon Account
https://amzn.to/2Q6DTXp

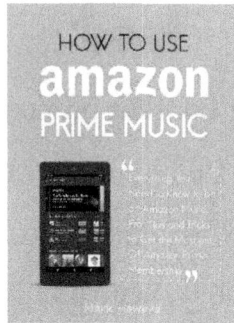

How to Use Amazon Prime Music: Everything
You Need to Know to be an Amazon Music
Pro, Tips and Tricks to Get the Most out Of
Amazon Prime Membership
https://amzn.to/2Oi1P8P

Printed in Dunstable, United Kingdom